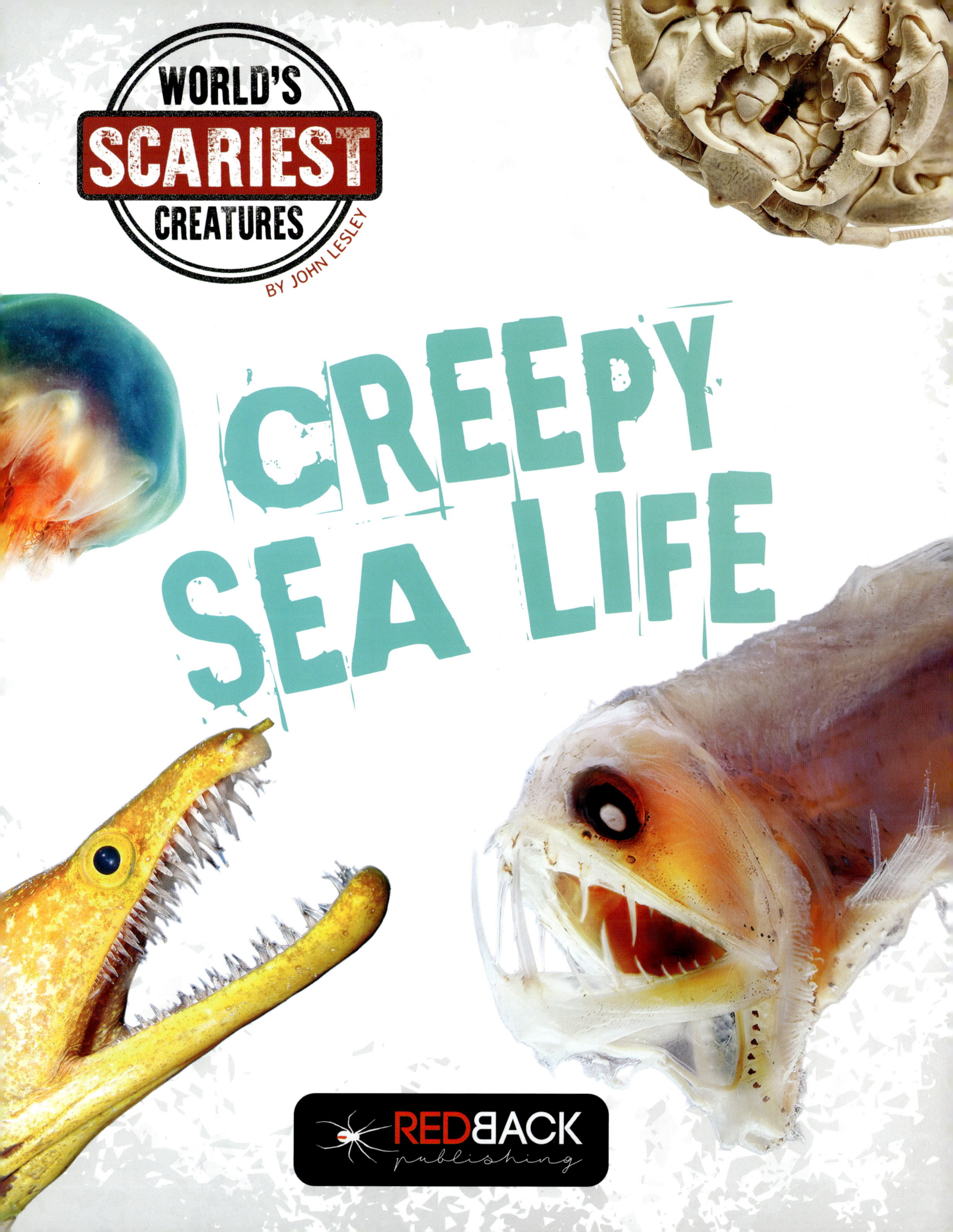
WORLD'S
SCARIEST
CREATURES
BY JOHN LESLEY
CREEPY
SEA LIFE
REDBACK
publishing

First published 2025 by
Redback Publishing
Suite 6, 13a Narabang Way,
Belrose NSW 2085
Australia

www.redbackpublishing.com
orders@redbackpublishing.com

ISBN 978-1-761401-71-8

A catalogue record for this book is available from the National Library of Australia

Author: John Lesley
Editors: Lucinda Dodds and Emma Dobinson
Designer: Redback Publishing
Original illustrations © Redback Publishing 2025
Originated by Redback Publishing

Acknowledgements
Abbreviations: l—left, r—right, b—bottom, t—top, c—centre, m—middle
We would like to thank the following for permission to reproduce photographs (images © Shutterstock unless otherwise stated)

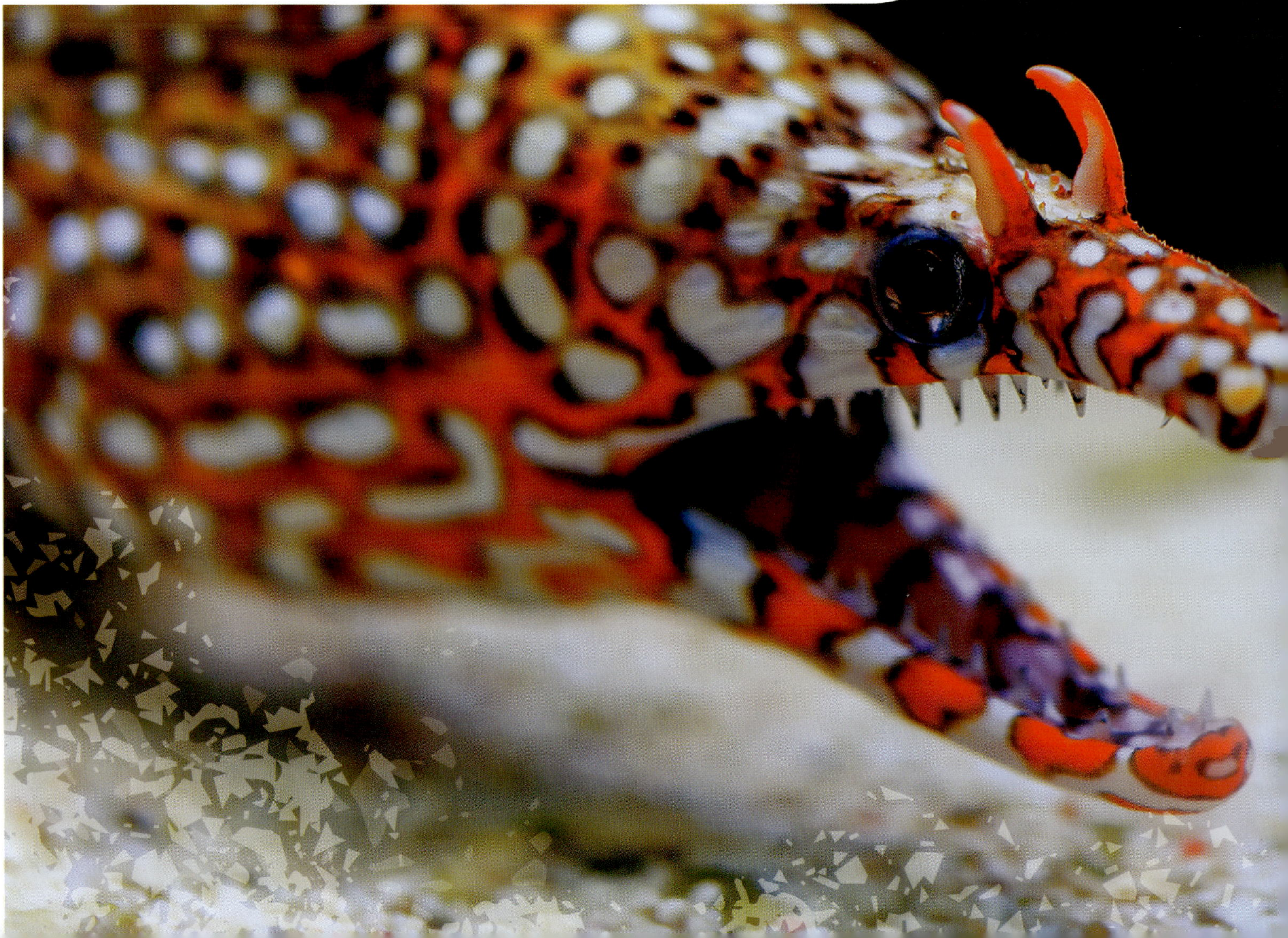

CONTENTS

UNDER THE WAVES

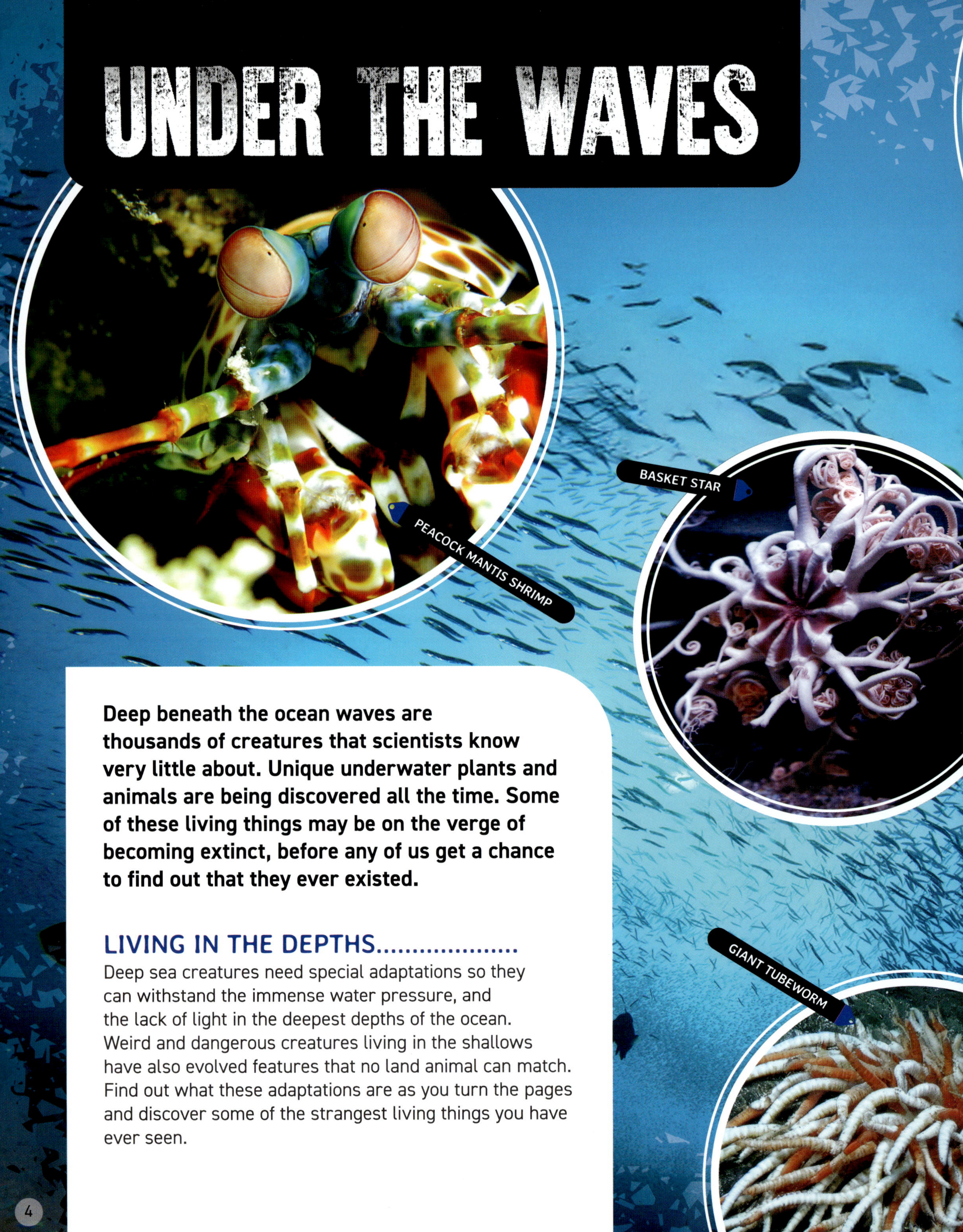

Deep beneath the ocean waves are thousands of creatures that scientists know very little about. Unique underwater plants and animals are being discovered all the time. Some of these living things may be on the verge of becoming extinct, before any of us get a chance to find out that they ever existed.

LIVING IN THE DEPTHS

Deep sea creatures need special adaptations so they can withstand the immense water pressure, and the lack of light in the deepest depths of the ocean. Weird and dangerous creatures living in the shallows have also evolved features that no land animal can match. Find out what these adaptations are as you turn the pages and discover some of the strangest living things you have ever seen.

FACT

In the deepest parts of the ocean, the pressure is over a thousand times more than it is on land.

Human bones would be crushed by this high pressure, but delicate fish and jellyfish have survived in the ocean depths for millions of years.

GIANT SQUID

Architeuthis dux

At over 13 metres long from the tip of its body to the last tentacle trailing in the water, the giant squid is a real, live monster. All squids are called cephalopods, which means they have a body which is basically a head and a foot combined, plus a lot of tentacles with suckers.

RARE

A live giant squid is rarely seen. We know about them mostly from the dead ones that wash up on beaches. They have eight arms, or tentacles, plus two extra-long feeding tentacles with sharp suckers that grab prey at a distance. The beak cuts the prey up and moves it into the mouth.

BIGGEST EYES

The giant squid's eyes are the largest of any living animal, at about 30 centimetres wide. They need big eyes to be able to see so they can hunt for food in the deep water where there is not much light.

FACT

Divers and small boats have been attacked by giant squids.

FACT FILE

Length: over 13 metres
Colour: brown/grey
Life span: about 5 years
Scientific name: *Architeuthis dux*

FACT

Delicious deep-fried calamari is made from little squids. You wouldn't want to eat calamari from their giant cousin!

JAPANESE SPIDER CRAB

Macrocheira kaempferi

The Japanese spider crab has the longest legs of any crab, and its whole body spans up to four metres across. It is not a spider, but it is distantly related to them, since both are in the animal group called arthropods. Instead of growing bones inside their bodies, arthropods all have hard outer coverings called exoskeletons. To camouflage itself, the young spider crab glues other small creatures onto its shell, mimicking the rocky seafloor.

TEN LEGS

The eight legs for walking are tipped with sharp claws. There are also an extra two legs at the front of the body that the crab uses for bringing food to its mouth, and for tearing open mollusc shells. Although the legs are long, spider crabs move slowly and do not scuttle around like spiders do.

FACT

Since they can't swim, spider crabs walk across the ocean floor.

FACT FILE

Width including legs: nearly 4 metres
Weight: up to 20 kilograms
Colour: orange and cream
Life span: perhaps up to 100 years
Scientific name: *Macrocheira kaempferi*

FACT

Females lay over a million eggs at a time.

BITE

Spider crabs are only dangerous if you get too close to their front claws. A nip from one of these claws can cause a lot of damage.

MORAY EEL

The moray eel hides in rock crevices in the sea, then dashes out to catch its prey. They have sharp teeth that can bite through the hand of anyone who tries to touch them.

Moral eels move like a snake in the water. The presence of a dorsal fin that goes all along the back is the best way to work out if the creature you are watching is a snake or a moray eel.

APEX PREDATOR

The moray eel is an apex predator in its habitat. Very few other marine creatures will dare to attack it. Those that do try to bite one will find that some moray eels have a toxic slime on their bodies as a protection against predators.

DOUBLE JAWS

Moray eels have double jaws, making their bite twice as unpleasant. The jaws that are at the back of the mouth shoot forward to grasp prey then pull it in.

BITTEN!

Anyone bitten by a moray eel will suffer extreme pain and bleeding. The worst bites can result in chunks being taken out of the skin. A moray eel brought to the surface in a fishing net is a dangerous catch, as it will still be able to bite.

FACT
Moray eels are a type of fish.
FACT
There are about 200 different types of moray eel.
FACT FILE
Length: over 3 metres
Colour: wide range of colours and patterns
Toxic: possibly
Life span: over 10 years

DEEP-SEA ANGLERFISH

Lophiiformes

FACT

Female anglerfish can be up to 10 times bigger than males!

Rather than having a body with a mouth, the anglerfish looks more like a mouth that grew a body as an afterthought. The mouth is so large that it can open to nearly half the body width.

LIGHTED LURE

Dangling at the top lip of the female is a long lure that lights up in the dark of the deep ocean. As little fish and crustaceans come to investigate, the huge mouth swallows them. The lure may also help to attract a mate. Although it is undeniably ugly, this sea monster is perfectly adapted to the dark of its deep-sea habitat.

MALE ANGLERFISH

The tiny male anglerfish fuses with the skin and blood vessels of the much larger female. They both live this way for life, making the job of searching for a mate again unnecessary for both of them.

FACT FILE

Length: from 2-100 centimetres long
Nickname: 'The Nightmare from the Abyss'
Colour: Wide range of colours, from bright yellow to greys and browns
Scientific name: Lophiiformes

FACT

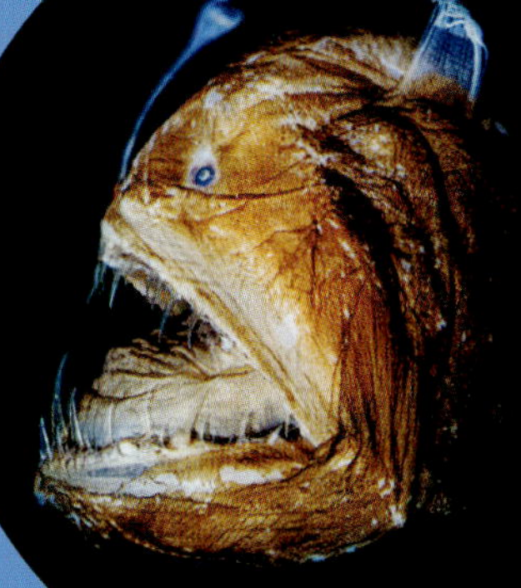

The lighted lure used by anglerfish is filled with bioluminescent bacteria.

FACT

Long, needle-like teeth ensure prey cannot escape.

VIPERFISH

Chauliodus

FACT

Viperfish are part of a group called dragonfish because of their hideous appearance.

Viperfish swim to the upper layers of the ocean at night to search for food. In the daytime, they dive down to a depth of two kilometres, where it is dark and they are safer from predators.

ADAPTATIONS

The viperfish teeth are sharp and so long that the mouth cannot close. A line of luminous spots along the body camouflage the viperfish by making it look like light coming into the water from the surface. The dorsal fin is also lit, but its purpose is to dangle over the head and lure prey into the spiked mouth.

FACT FILE

Length: between 6-30 centimetres
Weight: under 10 grams
Colour: iridescent grey
Life span: between 15-30 years
Scientific name: *Chauliodus*

FACT

Viperfish have the longest teeth in proportion to their head of any known fish!

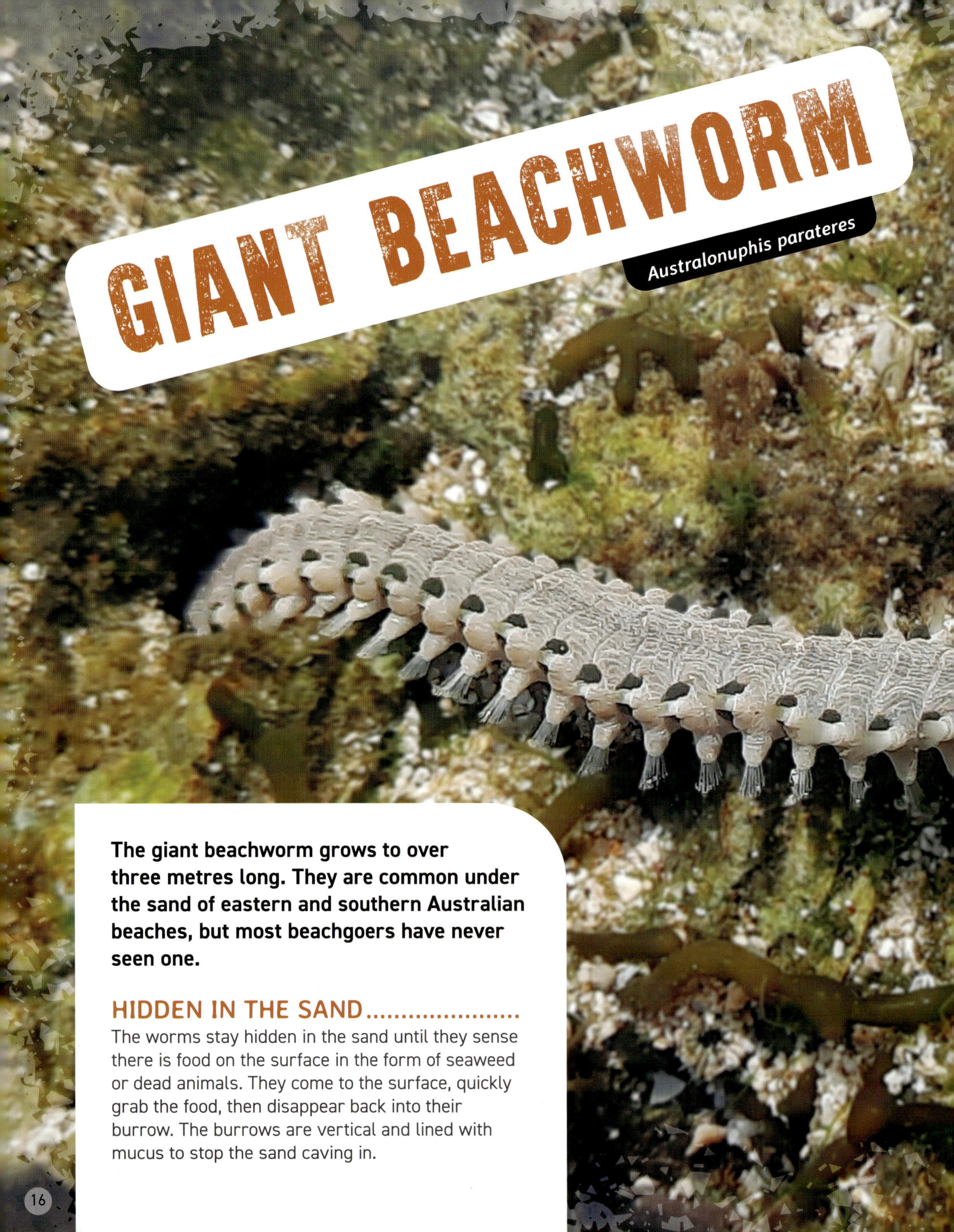

GIANT BEACHWORM

Australonuphis parateres

The giant beachworm grows to over three metres long. They are common under the sand of eastern and southern Australian beaches, but most beachgoers have never seen one.

HIDDEN IN THE SAND

The worms stay hidden in the sand until they sense there is food on the surface in the form of seaweed or dead animals. They come to the surface, quickly grab the food, then disappear back into their burrow. The burrows are vertical and lined with mucus to stop the sand caving in.

FACT FILE

Length: up to 3 metres
Width: up to 1.5 centimetres
Colour: brown body and legs
Scientific name: *Australonuphis parateres*

FACT

If you rub a piece of meat across wet sand, you may see a beachworm come up to take it.

FACT

Beachworms are a favourite bait used for fishing.

STARGAZER FISH

Uranoscopid

FACT

Instead of chasing prey, they suck fish into their mouths like a vacuum!

FACT

Stargazers have both venom and electric shocks!

Stargazer fish lie in wait on the seabed, ready to grab and swallow anything that wanders near them.

ADAPTATIONS

They have evolved to have eyes that sit on top of their flattened head, and a mouth that faces upwards. Some have a lure that looks like a wriggling worm and that attracts fish to swim almost straight into the stargazer's mouth. Just in case prey thinks it can swim away, the stargazer can deliver an electric shock to stop them moving. And as if that weren't enough, stargazers also have venomous spines near their gills.

FACT FILE

Length: the longest up to 70 centimetres long
Colour: colours to camouflage the fish on the seabed
Weight: largest grow to 9 kilograms
Nickname: 'The Electric Grave'

LION'S MANE JELLYFISH

Cyanea capillata

A lion's mane jellyfish can grow to be over two metres wide and have tentacles that are over 30 metres long, but most are smaller, with tentacles of less than 10 metres in length.

ADAPTATIONS

The tentacles are full of stingers and they hang in the water, waiting to trap food. The body is a reddish orange colour, and the long tentacles are translucent, making them difficult to see.

FACT FILE

Length: up to 30 metres
Colour: red, orange, translucent
Venomous: yes
Life span: 1 year
Scientific name: *Cyanea capillata*

FACT

Leatherback turtles feed on these jellyfish and seem to be immune to the stings.

FACT

Even broken tentacle pieces can sting and cause extreme pain.

GIANT PACIFIC OCTOPUS

Enteroctopus dofleini

FACT

The female does not eat after laying and protecting her eggs. She then dies from starvation.

The biggest octopus in the world is the giant Pacific octopus, which grows to the astounding size of over four metres from arm to arm.

SUCKERS

The suckers on the arms trap prey and bring it to the mouth, where the sharp beak cuts it up. With so many suckers on its eight long arms, the giant Pacific octopus can make sure quite large prey does not escape.

EGGS

They only breed once in their life, and at that time the female might produce many thousands of eggs. Most of these are eaten by predators.

FACT FILE

Width: over 4 metres
Colour: red/brown
Venomous: yes
Life span: 5 years
Scientific name: *Enteroctopus dofleini*

Octopuses are very intelligent.

VENOM

Some divers have reported being attacked by a giant Pacific octopus. Their bite contains venom that can make a person very sick.

GIANT ISOPOD

Bathynomus giganteus

If you are scared of cockroaches, the giant isopods will not be your favourite creature. Although they are both arthropods, the marine isopods are more closely related to crabs than cockroaches.

LIFESTYLE

The giant isopod can grow to 50 centimetres long and weigh nearly two kilograms. They have multiple body segments and seven pairs of legs. They hunt for food and also eat dead animals that they find. Isopods might bite, so keep your fingers away if you don't want them to be chewed.

FACT FILE

Length: up to 50 centimetres
Colour: brown, white
Life span: not known for certain, but may be many years
Scientific name: *Bathynomus giganteus*

Giant isopods can live kilometres deep in the ocean.

FACT

They roll themselves into a ball if a predator threatens them.

SEA SCORPION

Jaekelopterus

Although it is called a sea scorpion, *Jaekelopterus* may have lived in rivers and lakes and not in the sea.

Sea scorpions are extinct so you don't have to worry about meeting one in the ocean. The biggest sea scorpion known to have ever existed was *Jaekelopterus*.

LIFESTYLE

This giant arthropod lived about 390 million years ago. It would have grown to nearly three metres long and had large jaws. Its pincers were used for feeding and were nearly half a metre wide.

FACT
Sea scorpion claws had teeth to tear prey into pieces.

PISTOL SHRIMP

Alpheidae

This shrimp may be tiny, but its weird skills are amazing. It has a snapping claw that masquerades as a gun, creating a bubble and shooting a shock wave through the water at over 50 kph. This causes a blast that stuns or kills its prey. If the pistol shrimp were scaled up to human size it would be a lethal monster.

SNAP!

The snapping noise of pistol shrimp can be so loud that it interferes with human sonar equipment used to investigate objects under the water.
The bubble produced by the pistol shrimp is very hot and surprisingly creates a tiny and temporary burst of light.

FACT

The shock wave comes from a click that lasts less than one millisecond.

FACT FILE

Length: up to 5 centimetres long
Nickname: 'The Underwater Assassin'; the snapping shrimp
Colour: brown, red
Scientific name: *Alpheidae*

FACT

The snapping claw is half the size of the whole body of the shrimp.

DEEP SEA GIGANTISM

GIGANTISM

Gigantism refers to a life form that naturally grows to be huge. The 30-metre-long blue whale is the biggest animal alive on our planet, but there are also other enormous sea creatures deep down in the ocean that are rarely seen.

The biggest creatures on Earth are aquatic for a reason. The water helps to support their shape. If they were on land, they could be crushed by their own mighty weight.

WHALE SHARK
PURPLE TUBE SPONGES
BLUE WHALE
MEGA CORAL

GLOSSARY

camouflage method of hiding by looking like the surroundings

cephalopod creature with a head and foot combined

DNA genetic material in the cells of living things

dorsal referring to the back of a living thing

exoskeleton hard outer shell that supports an animal's shape and internal organs

gigantism type of growth pattern that produces a very large animal

molluscs invertebrates that include snails, oysters and octopuses

mucus substance like slime

scuttle run quickly with short steps

verge edge

INDEX